A Girl with Nine Lives

CHYNA DOLL

Copyright © 2017 Chyna Doll.

All rights reserved. No part of this book may be used or reproduced by any means, graphic, electronic, or mechanical, including photocopying, recording, taping or by any information storage retrieval system without the written permission of the author except in the case of brief quotations embodied in critical articles and reviews.

WestBow Press books may be ordered through booksellers or by contacting:

WestBow Press
A Division of Thomas Nelson & Zondervan
1663 Liberty Drive
Bloomington, IN 47403
www.westbowpress.com
1 (866) 928-1240

Because of the dynamic nature of the Internet, any web addresses or links contained in this book may have changed since publication and may no longer be valid. The views expressed in this work are solely those of the author and do not necessarily reflect the views of the publisher, and the publisher hereby disclaims any responsibility for them.

Any people depicted in stock imagery provided by Thinkstock are models, and such images are being used for illustrative purposes only.
Certain stock imagery © Thinkstock.

ISBN: 978-1-5127-6990-6 (sc)
ISBN: 978-1-5127-6989-0 (e)

Library of Congress Control Number: 2016921301

Print information available on the last page.

WestBow Press rev. date: 1/10/2017

Preface

Over the years, I had to accept some of the aspects of my life - the drug abuse, being molested, domestic violence and rape. The time had come were each situation had to be addressed by me in order to move on. In writing my thoughts, which started out as a diary and after a while, I realized that expressing my experiences was healthy for my soul. It relieves some of the stresses and the pain. As I look back on my life and as I write about it, I relive it over and over again. I recreate it all over the foibles of others as time went on so I can forgive. By writing about my story, sharing my secrets and some of my buried most deeply, hidden thoughts has released a journey of freedom. I pushed so much in the back of my mind for year shopping to deal with it at a later while I lived my life for now. Dealing with it now I recall how ashamed I was to tell anyone. I was embarrassed while writing about it every day. I found working through the past event and conflicts bare a cleansing to my soul. It is and can be an effective method of treatment emotionally and physically. Forgiving myself and others took a long time as the domestic violence is concerned. I still live in fear every day not knowing if that man was or is ever caught.

In order to maintain anonymity of those in my memoirs, I have changed individual names, identifying characteristics, recreated events, locals, and place of residence, occupations and all related conversations.

I pray that my story may help others reach out to someone who may be in trouble. You don't have to be silent anymore. Find someone you can trust and tell them what is going on, because there is help today.

It was a hot summer day in June of 1996. It was the day I married my best friend. It was a beautiful wedding that every woman dreamed of because you get to share it with your family and friends.

I had all my sisters in my wedding. It was awesome! Then there was the end of the day, when it's all over, it's just you and your husband. You have to be your own person and keep family from interfering because it will not last if you allow them in. I don't worry about what people say or think because when it's all over, they are with who they want to be with and you are all alone.

I thought when we made those vows to God that it would last forever. I have no regrets though. He was a good man. I only wished it could've worked out and he took his vows to me more seriously. I realize today that nothing last forever. He asked me if I wanted a house or a wedding. At the time none of my sisters were married and my mom had lost her sight in one eye. So, I wanted to give her something to remember and I chose the wedding.

In the end it left me with great memories. I have never cared much about what people thought of me. People will try to give you advice but don't really mean it. You are alone while they are with whom they want to be. My mom always said, *"If a man don't want you, move on. What is the sense of hanging on to someone that doesn't care about you any more?"*

It was the grace of God that kept me because it was the hardest decision I had to make. We put ourselves in through these situations but God prepares us by using our lessons to make you a stronger person. I wish him the best in life and may God bless his journey. I have moved on. God has bless me in so many ways that I can't explain. I am so grateful and thankful for the person I am today and where I am in my life.

Our mom is the one we turn to when things get rough. Her love is unconditional. She teaches us through her example, and as long as there are mothers who care very much, her love will shine through in all the lives she touches. God's tender mercies gave me a father, sisters and a brother but God in his infinite wisdom, blessed me with his loving mercies.

FAMILY

I grew up in the "Projects" with four siblings- three sisters and a brother who was a good looking guy and a ladies' man until he married, I love him to death, and we are very close.

We grew up in a community where everyone knew each other and respected each other's family members. We never disrespected anyone's parents. We played outside and hung our laundry out on clothes lines. We had benches to sit on and even left our doors unlocked. It was a family-oriented community.

For a while, my mom was a housewife-a beautiful woman inside and out. After my mom separated from my dad, she worked every day to keep food on the table and clothes on our backs. She carries a spirit that draws people to want to meet and talk to her. She is still my best friend today and has lived to see all her children to reach their 60's, which is a blessing.

My oldest sister, Leslie, took care of all of us. She

made sure we ate dinner, had our baths, and did our homework then got ready for bed. Then she started her own family, had two boys and one daughter- her daughter which I love with all my heart. She is my favorite niece. I remember one day, when she was about five, we were on the porch. She looked up at me and said, *"You think you cute?"*

And I looked at her, heartbroken, and then answered, *"Why you say that?"*

She said, *"Because you do!"*

I answered her, *"no I don't"*.

I always had a complex about my looks. I was so skinny. I just didn't like the way I looked. Back in those days, I thought you had to be light-skinned which was in during those times. You were call red-bonedwomen; my sister Leslie was tall, skinny and light-skinned. She dressed well, kept her hair done! She was sharp back in her time, her girlfriends too. One day, she brought her girlfriend and her girlfriend's boyfriend home. The guy had started a conversation with my mom and when they finished talking, he turned out to be related to us. His mother was my father's sister. How about that! He was a good- looking chocolate tall guy. I said too bad *"you are my cousin."* I was young and fresh, and he said, *"You are something else."* I remember he took me downstairs and brought me an ice cream cone off the truck. I never

A Girl with Nine Lives

saw him again – it was some years later, I believe, when I was all grown up.

My next to the oldest sister is Jesse. She was my favorite. She would press my hair, buy me clothes, and take me shopping. In return, I would babysit her children, take them to the nursery, and pick them up. She had three daughters and one son. I was around my nieces and nephews all the time. I would sleep all day and go out at night. I was always running in the street – they called me the black sheep of the family. My sisters are two years apart. We were never really close but I loved all my sisters and my brother is my favorite.

Now, the sister over me is Sarah. She was tall, light-skinned with long pretty brown hair. She always dressed fine, wore beautiful clothes but her attitude made her look so ugly. She always thought that she was better than us. She didn't even know how much I admired her. She was mean and horrible to me. But after a while, I got used to her nasty attitude. We used to fight all the time. I remember in high school, I used to sneak and wearher clothes. It was one cold day, she caught me outside wearing her coat – it was a tan, leather coat with fur on it. She caught me outside of school and made me take it off. I walked home in the cold with no coat. Now, let me tell you how mean she was because the next day, she let her girlfriend where the same coat that she made me takes off in the cold. She had a little handsome son. I used to babysit for her, and she lived a secret life. We all make bad choices and mistakes in our lives, and so did I. But, I never judged anyone because my life was so unbalanced. The only person we have to answer to is God. None of us are perfect!

She wanted to be in the lime light. She couldn't sing for nothing, but she thought that she could. She used to tell on me all the time but always wanted to hang out with me. She used to treat my mom like dirt. After she left home, during that time in my life I disliked her. She used to tell people that she was abused, and she never was. If you know my mom, she is the sweetest woman in the world. You know some people just want to be in the lime light or want attention, and would do anything to get it! Sad but that was her. Though she was beautiful, she thought her attitude didn't stink. She wore a mask and didn't even know it, or maybe she did. She used to molest me at night, for a long time. I never mentioned it because my mom being in such denial about things, she probably wouldn't have believed me, and I was already humiliated enough. Even now, people don't listen to their children because for one, it is a family member that hurts them. I didn't say anything but she would do it a couple of times a week, at the time I couldn't understand what was happening, but I let her do it, she would get in my bed, and start fondling me. She would say just before we go to bed, "Tonight is the night again" then I would let her. Maybe she was using me as an experiment. I wasn't sure what that was about, so I let her do it; I was too embarrassed and humiliated.

I have this message called the Mask that are people that wear so many different masks because they are not confident enough to be themselves, or they worry about what people think about them, that if may be, they're not themselves, people may accept them more. How heavy are your burdens? We will never know what makes someone tic, or what goes into making someone's character, emotions, love, hate or anger. What mask is on display, what emotions will replay, happiness, sadness, love and anger or disappointment, over and over no one can tell the facial mask is worn, so heavy- how are your burdens hidden, very well not revealing, a camouflage of failing no one will never know only one person.

Yes, our higher power - God Almighty. How you become a master in disguise. God made every one different, because if we all are alike, the world would be in trouble. Just be yourself, love yourself, be proud of who you are. We all are a child of God. It doesn't matter how long you live. It's what you leave behind that does. Coming together is a beginning key and it is a working process. Coming together is success whether it's a personal or a business relationship. If we come together and work together with honesty and clarity, then we can stay together, with risk factors and meet our goals. I need people that will support and encourage my dreams. Some people will, you must move on and leave the ones that don't behind. Then there are people that try to be your friend, will just call to see how you are doing but don't really want to know. So, why ask? I had a few of them just wanted to know what was going on and didn't really care about the person as long as there was something in it for them.

Grammar School

*G*rammar school, it was differently peer pressure. I really didn't like myself because I thought I was ugly, my self-esteem was low, and I wasn't ready for sex at that time. There was this boy that liked me in the seventh grade, he was cute, well-built and all the girls liked him. There was this one girl who was jealous of me and wanted to fight me because that guy liked me instead of her. He was a very popular guy. He used to come and talk to me but I think back then, I was afraid of the boys because all the girls my age was already having sex so I guess that's why I didn't fit in. This particular girl, her name was Sandy. She would always get my face. She was very jealous because she would always see Ben talking to me and she was ready to give up the sex to him, and I wasn't. So one day in school, I heard that Sandy wanted to fight Princess, and I thought to myself, *"Really, what did I do to her anyway?"*

After school, she came and jumped in my face. You

know, when you're scared, you get the strength to beat that other person up. I was young and I was scared. When she came in my face, I beat her up. Once you let someone know that they are not going to bully you, they will back off. You don't have to put up with their craziness or let them punk you, they will respect you. So after the fight we had, she spoke to me every day, and I wasn't scared of her anymore.

In the eighth grade, it was so bad. I used to be embarrassed sometimes. The kids would come to school with new shoes or sneakers. There were five of us. My mom did the best she could, but when we had holes in the bottom of our shoes or sneakers, we had to tear off a piece of cardboard and put it in our shoe and go on to school. I always said, when I grow up and get a job, when I can take care of myself, I will buy me as many pairs of shoes and sneakers that I want, and that's exactly what I did. I did use to where my sisters' shoes to school but their feet was so big and mine was so small that I had to put tissue in them so that they would fit. When I graduated grammar school, I got into high school. It was very scary. You know that is when more peer pressure really sets in. You want people to like you, you want to fit in, but everyone is not going to accept you. Everyone is not going to like you either, that's life. I had a few friends. The ones that had been pretty good.

Then, I tried out for the cheerleading squad. I made it, which was the best time I had in high school. I was in the 9th grade and my sister Sarah was in the 11th. People that know us knew we were sisters. But when people that did not know us found out that Sarah was my sister, they couldn't believe it. I understood because we were like night and day. She was tall, light-skinned, with long, gorgeous hair, and wore beautiful clothes. But she had a messed up attitude. I believe she was embarrassed of me because I didn't dress like her. However, I made it through anyway. I mingled more with her classmate's then mine because I was a cheerleader. I loved being a cheerleader.

In the 11th grade, I wasn't interested in anyone in my school. One of the guys on the football team, Dan, used to say we were brother and sister. He's gone today though – may rest in peace. One of his friends didn't go to our school but was always around. He was tall, had brown skin, real bowed legs, good-looking, smart, and wore glasses. I found out he didn't have a girlfriend, so I inquired about this guy and he lived in the projects across town. He really didn't like me, so I pursued him.

My girlfriend lived in his projects across town, and I used to visit her and then I wanted to visit him. She would say, *"Girl you are crazy"*.

I would say to her, *"stop being so scary, just come with me over to his building."*

When we got there, it was girls outside, looking like *who are they?* I said, *"I am looking for Booboo?"*

The girls said, *"He doesn't have a girlfriend"*.

I said, *"Not yet!"* then I walked in his building, I was scared to death and didn't know what I was going to say. When I arrive at his door, he wasn't there. His mother answered, and I introduced myself to her.

You know how you get to the sister first to get to the brother? Well, I didn't have to do that I got him on my own. I said he going to have one now, and that's just what happened. I laugh to myself. When we started talking on the phone, we became close. He was my first love for very long time, and we had a baby at a young age.

Then he started dating a woman from another High school, who also was a cheerleader. Asiawas her name, she was in the same grade as I was, and when our schools played against each other in football and basketball, he would never show up, and I couldn't understand why at the time.

I loved being a cheerleader. In the 11th grade, I found out he was cheating on me with this woman. You know MEN, they are going to deny it at first, but eventually, it came to light. In my senior year when we both got pregnant. He denied both babies in the beginning, but at the end of the day, I though he was just scared because he had two babies on the way. But his mom and sisters were happy for me. They liked me a lot. They said I was good for him. I even gave his mother a nick name. I called her Nana, and then everyone started calling her by that name. I became very much part of his family.

Back in high school, when young girls get pregnant, they had a program that you can take your classes from three in the afternoon till six in the evening and graduate with your senior class. And that's what we both did. It was very uncomfortable because both of us are in the evening classes. For a long time, I couldn't believe Asia was pregnant, because it took so long for her to show, but I did immediately!

When we saw each other for the first time in the evening classes, we acknowledged one another and both believed that we were pregnant by the same man. It was a hurting feeling.

In May 1973, she gave birth to a baby boy. Two weeks later, I gave birth to the most beautiful baby girl that changed my whole life forever. I was able to graduate with my senior class that year and I was very proud of myself after all that drama started.

My daughter's grandmother took very good care of

her and loved her very much. There wasn't a book on how to be a mother at a young age or any age really. You learn how to love this little person and protect them as much as you can, teach them right from wrong and then, after they grow up, they will always be your baby but then they grow into adulthood.

Some others don't know how to show affection, like they don't hug their kids. They don't talk or listen to them. I'm grown and I still want to be hugged and be told that I'm loved from my mom. It wasn't easy being a young mother but I watched my sisters on how to be a mother. Everyone has their own way of doing things. You might have yours and I have mine, but it all comes together at the end. It may not be right but I tried. When my daughter was about six months old, I got a job at a hospital so that I can take care of her. Her father and I were in and out of our relationship because of the other woman. I stayed at his mom's sometimes, most of the times, but we always fought. My daughter must have been about 7 months old when one particular evening, we stayed the night at his mom's and he was out in the street somewhere. We had planned to marry one day. We had the marriage license and I loved this man, so there was no way he was going to be married to the other woman.

It was a late Saturday night when his mom was at

work. My daughter and I were watching TV. The phone rang, I answered, "Hi, how are you?" Even before all that happened, his sister's friends put her up to start a fight with me, because her brother likes me and not Asia. So, one day after school, everyone came running to me stating that there was a crowd of people outside waiting for me to have this fight that I knew nothing about. When I got outside, the crowd followed me and my girlfriend home to this big parking lot, so I stopped, turned around and said *"Let's just get this over with,"*

I beat his sister up, but next thing I knew they jumped to me, and beat me up. But guess what, he still was cheating on the both of us. When I had enough of his crap, it was over. I had black eyes and a busted lip. I had enough of the garbage with him. Once I made up my mind about something or someone, I am done. It's over, let it go, and move on.

Finally, I let him go, and moved on. Enough was enough. His family loved my child unconditionally. She could do no wrong in her nana's eyes. His sister tried to tell my daughter that I didn't want her, that's why she was living with them. When she was old enough to understand what I went through, I explain to her I was going to have a nervous break down, at that time in my life, and instead of putting her in the system, her grandmother took care of her until I got better. She understood after that.

Few hours later, I get a call from Ben stating what happen what you do, I told him to leave me alone. This wasn't my house I try to respect nana's house but this women wouldn't let me. I tried to be honest with her but she kept calling back, saying I wasn't his wife, but I know her girlfriend put her up to that. She kept calling saying what she wanted to do to me, I told her, *come on*. When she arrived at the house and I opened the door, I punched her in the face. The house they lived in, you have to come in and walk all the way to the back, I dragged her butt from the inside of the hallway, down the stairs then outside to the curve and beat her up. When Ben came home, my daughter and I were in the bed and he started arguing with me over her. It was a cold night, and it was freezing outside. We ended up arguing and fighting because Asia and I had a fight because of him. I was in my nightclothes, and I will never forget he wouldn't let me take my daughter. I ran out the house down the street in my nightclothes jumped in a cab and went to my mom's house. When I arrived at my mom's, she said, *"**Oh my,** what happen? Where's the baby? Oh my"*, I explained to her what happened with Asia and I, and then my baby daddy came home fighting me because I beat his girlfriend up and he didn't like it.

The next morning, my mom and I went back to his house. His mom was there to get my daughter. His mom told him that he had no business putting his hands on me and to give me my baby even though she was both of ours. I told his mom he got upset because I tore up the marriage license, and that I would never marry him because once a man hits you and they say, *baby I'm sorry* and when they get upset again, they will hit you again and again and again. I was very young but I wasn't having it. I loved this man to death but we couldn't make it work so after some years I had to let it go.

Drugs and Domestic Violence

When the depression started settling in, I had been working at the hospital about a year before I was laid off. I couldn't find another job for a while. It was hard so I got on public assistance. That was when I started smoking weed, and taking pills. In school, I was introduced to dope but I couldn't handle it because it was a down high and it always made me sick.

Then I got introduced to cocaine. I loved the way cocaine made me feel when I was sad and depressed. I would get high and the pain would subside, but once the high is gone, the pain is still there and then you have to deal with it, and want more and more.

Life is a struggle, living is a learning experience, and life is what you make it. I was still a young mother with a baby. Well, I used to wake up and say to myself, who *is Princess? Does anyone know who she is?*

I always had a complex about myself, my looks, how I dressed, I thought at that time that clothes made a person but I found out that it doesn't. You know you try to fit in the crowd and doing the things they do, and you still don't fit in. I didn't have to go to bed with someone else's husband for the record, believe me I was accused, one of my family members accuse me of sleeping with her husband, to get what I wanted; so let's make that clear. Just because I was the black sheep, people thought that I did. One day, I get a phone call from a relative that lived in Maryland, we had been friends for along time, she would babysit my daughter, she would feed her, and we would talk on the phone for hours at night.

This particular night, I received the phone call. I was devastated. I was hurt because she accused me of sleeping around with her man. You know when people call you up and tell you things that's really not about you, at the end of the day, it's the messenger that passed on the message, trying to turn the heat off of them. So, I went to her house and I confronted her husband in front of her, he just laid there. He didn't admit it and he didn't deny, but I let him know that this is my family and he knows that I never slept with him no matter what he gave me. So, after that, I left her house and didn't hear from her for a long time. A couple years later, she called me and apologized, it was too late. The damage was done. I was hurt, and it took me a long time to forgive her.

Today I still love her like I was never accused. I can forgive but I can't forget. While I was in the streets, I did a lot of dirt and hurt a lot of people, but not to someone in my family that I would regret later on. I just wanted to set the record straight about that life with the drugs, being molested, raped; having guns put to my head I am still here to tell my story. It was only God's grace and his mercy that I'm still here, because God take care of babies and fools, and I was definitely a fool.

I love all my nieces and nephews, I used to be so embarrassed to come around them when I was down and out. They never embarrassed me, they all just loved me. I would try to spend time with them take them to New York, to the parks and then go back to my own self in the streets. I use to listen to them when they talk to me, never did I judge them or they judged me. Back then, I might not have had anything to offer to them but my ears and whenever they needed to talk, I would listen. I never had a role model in my life, it was very hard and difficult, but I got by. I did know how to pray and ask God to keep me, even though I was doing wrong. God kept me because I had 9 lives, and I am here to tell my story. Hallelujah!!!!!!

Chyna Doll

I have a cousin named Silky Smooth, he is my best friend and still my best friend today, I still call him for advice or just to say hello, he has been my back bone throughout the years. I am so grateful for him, he has a brother that was jealous of our friendship.

Another cousin set me up one day and told me his sister wanted to see me. I said ok, then I felt that little voice inside, saying don't go, but I said to myself he won't hurt me. Well we get to the sister's house and she wasn't there, I said where is she, oh she will be here any minute, I got scared, he started chasing me around the house, finally he got me on the bed no matter how much I cried and screamed he took my pants off and said, I wanted you for a long time and this is the only way I can get it. When he was finish, I got up put my pants on, crying at the same time, he then took me home, and I walked in the house like nothing had happen to me. I kept saying to myself, girl you just got raped? I looked at my family, I wanted to say something but couldn't. Then I thought would they even believe me? So, I walked to the bathroom and sat on the toilet, crying softly so no one could hear me, I didn't want to feel more frustrated and furious if she didn't believe me. So I sat in the tub and just let the water run, we didn't have a shower so I just sat there just scrubbing my skin and crying out but no one could hear me, but God. I call silky and told him what happened, he said he was so sorry he felt bad for me, but there wasn't anything he could really do but comfort me. I appreciated that because I didn't want to hear anything negative.

A few years later I saw him at his nieces wedding he look at me and said, you still mad at me? Girl get over it! I wanted to slap his face off. I prayed all the time, sometimes it helped, sometimes it didn't, but today pray is power. I do believe in God's word and couldn't have made it without him. I stayed angry a lot; I didn't know how to deal with the pain I was feeling. Sometime you can have someone who we can really talk to, many times we need our space and opportunities to vent our anger, frustrations or dissatisfactions. My emotions do not release them if a loved one would take their frustration out on me. I must try not to take it personally. I must learn how to accept other's feelings, support their expressions and how they feel. My mom always said Princess, think before you speak; it's not what you say; it's how you say. If I say something that is painful and angry, I must separate the truth and what is real, if and when we get angry we should take a walk or will probably have a lot less to fight about. This is how I feel today I still have a lot of anger in me I need to release. I am really outraged, irritated, furious and miserable, because some other things that happened to me, I just pushed them way back in my mind and didn't deal with it. Next question is if they would believe me, and if they didn't that would hurt even more. So, sometimes you just have to push things in the back until you're ready to deal with them, so I went through so much pain and agony. I didn't know writing was a healing process, so I started writing how I felt each and every day. I wrote what people did to me and as time went on I started feeling better. God brought me through the storms, those dark nights when I couldn't tell anyone what I had been through, what just happened to me, I was embarrassed. When, I was about 21, I had started dating this drug dealer and he was so fine. I never thought in my wildest dreams that he liked me, I think it was more about the sex and the drugs, because he had already had kids. Even though I wasn't looking for a relationship, it was just about the drugs and sex. Big daddy was tall, dark, handsome and well-dressed doing his own thing. I was shocked when he asked to take me out and then we had sex. I really liked this guy but I knew he didn't want anything serious, I wind up getting pregnant. I was so scared. One day I said to him out of the blue "would you want to have any more kids?" He said no and I then realized what I had to do. I had an abortion and I never told big daddy till this day that I was pregnant. Only my

A Girl with Nine Lives

cousin that went through the abortion process with me because I was so afraid, I couldn't trust anyone else at the time, she worked at the hospital where I had the procedure. She was afraid for me because I was so far gone that I had to go through the labor. She was worrying about what to tell my mom if something happened to me in the process. I told her don't worry it will be fine. I would tell my mom that I just needed a cleaning, that's what they call a D&C, in medical terms. The day I got home I was in so much pain, I laid on the couch, my mom was at work, my sister Sara and her son was home and my daughter. Sarah and I got into an argument because she was feeding her son and my baby was hungry and she wouldn't feed my daughter. Mom was at work, so I got up start arguing with her. I was so stressed out just over life and things with my baby daddy that I just wanted to die. I had a friend that lived across the court at the time she was selling pills called sea bras and codeine. I said to her someone wanted to buy a 10 on 10 she said wow that's great. That's all I'll be right over to get them I wrote her a letter and asked her not to read it until the next day and she said okay. I left her house and went back home, picked up my daughter, hugged her so tight, she was the cutest little baby girl you have ever saw. I put her down and I went in the bathroom, looked in the mirror, I took the pills and came back into the kitchen and got on the phone. I can't remember who I called. The next thing I heard was Sara say mom look at her she's on the phone nodding and that's all I remember. The next time I woke up I was in the hospital they had pumped my stomach. I guess God said it's not your time I'm still working on you, my mom told me the doctor said they had just got me there in time or I wouldn't be here to tell you this story. Today I am truly blessed and grateful that I didn't die because that's not what I really wanted to do. I know God has a plan for me for my life. I was so happy to see my little girl after I got out the hospital, she would have never known her mother if I had died. Thank you God for saving my life again! Today my life has changed for the better. I love life, I love the woman I become. After my suicide attempt I realized that I was taking the easy way out.

After my baby daddy I dated a friend that taught me how to skate. We went to school together, he wanted to learn how to drive a tractor trailer. I introduced him to my brother-in-law and he learned. Larry and my daughter had a special bond. We went to high school together he was a really good, nice guy but he couldn't handle me with the drugs. He didn't know what to do with me, he said, but one day he smacked my face and that was the end of our relationship. For some reason that night he said his car drove him to my house and when he arrive there they told him what had happen to me? He said he couldn't understand what made him come to my house, when he got in his car it drove him right to my house for some reason. At the end of the day he still loved me, and he will hold a special place in my heart always. Today we are still friends. That night I tried to take my life, he was on his way to the skating rink, he said he couldn't understand what made him drive to my house that night; I guess it was God, telling him that something was wrong with me. We still skate today, which is great exercise and lots of fun; all of us old timers still meet up sometimes.

I started dating this Bouncer and Larry, although I didn't know how close they were, Larry, thought I was trying to get back at him, I asked the Bouncer, why he never told me that they were close like brothers; he stated that he knew I wouldn't have dated him and he was right. It's something to have two men in love with the same woman, I didn't know how to handle it, but I fell in love with the bouncer. We became very close. He was a construction worker too, you know that type of work you get laid off sometimes. Well a couple of years went by he came home and said to me he got laid off. I believe it was his pride because when he told me I was working and when you and your partner is in a

Chyna Doll

relationship at least I thought; when one get laid off the other one pick up the slack, well bouncer left and I slammed the door behind him, but before he left I tried to explain to him how this works, but he hated to hear the truth, it was his pride so we broke up he broke my heart and I never took him back after that. Once I got over him I was done he married another women after I said no and wouldn't take him back. But he would always call and stay in touch, God bless his soul may he R.I.P. My dear friend you will always hold a special place in my heart so, again looking for love in all the wrong places. Some women today feel like you have to have a man to be complete that is so not true, we are strong black women. We may go through tough times but God has our backs and at the end of the tunnel there is always a light we just have to pray that God will bring us through. I have to remember, everyone makes mistakes in life. It is a learning experience, but you shape up and keep moving, you make every effort to add to your faith, goodness, knowledge, and self-control. To self-control preservation and to present a chins those qualities increase in measures they will keep me from inefficient and unproductive in my life and knowledge what is most valuable is not what we have in our lives but who we have in our lives free your heart from hatred, forgive, free your mind from where Rest most never happen, list simply and appreciate what you gave and expect less then, I search my heart and found the creator of heaven and earth seen and unseen blessed me with the knowledge of wisdom and understanding, remember Life and gratitude heal everything we do things from the soul river moving in you and your way with the power of love overcome the love of power. Love is dangerous its deep affection an emotion, sexual passion greatly cherished. Today women and men have a choice, even in only the choice we have is the attitude in which we embrace each moment. Everything of life is a blessing from God, each breath is a prayer, in every whisper, every sight is a portrait, in every conversation is a verse, every day is a blessing. Angels opened up their eyes, rest in the eyes or family and friends, God reads to me every day a raindrop, a baptism of breeze and God blows in life into our body and every meal is the nourishment of the spirit is my testimony. I've learned that you can tell a lot about a person by how they handle such relationships with their parents. I've also learned making a living that you can tell a lot about a person how they handle such relationships with their parents. I've also learned making a living is not the same; we listen to the same all lines, follow down same old role and hope we can change. I listen to what people and hear something else; they are not really saying anything.

I thank God today for giving me another chance I truly pray that people can accept me as the woman I am today. It helps me heal somewhat when I think about sex the drug use and what I put my daughter through. I am grateful to be here today to write and talk about my experience and pray that my book will help someone out there that is reading it. There is so much peer pressure today, young and old women we have choices today not like back in time when my mother did whatever she had to keep our family together. I'm not knocking her generation but times have changed. I feel this time in my life I'm not where I should be or may be it just takes time. A couple of months before I got married I went to the doctor because I was having this pain in my stomach, I called my gynecologists, and told her the pain was bad we can't wait until after my wedding. Well in February 1996 I had a bowel obstruction, this is another time God saved my life, I woke up with unbearable pain, went to the doctor and that she couldn't see everything that was going on inside me. Now my mom and husband at the time, was in the waiting area when she came out and spoke to them. The doctor said let's do an exploratory, which is when they go through the navel. She had to call in a specialist because she couldn't get in through my Navel. So the specialist came in and did what he had

A Girl with Nine Lives

to do and saved my life again. After my recovery he came into my room he said, "Miss, I've never in my life seen anything like I saw in you. What was wrong? I asked the doctor. He explains that I was full of bowel that a thin shield grew over the bowel and that's why the poison didn't get into my bloodstream. I was so shocked that happened to me and thanked God that I went to the doctor or I wouldn't have been here to get married that June. Everything happens for a reason. So, your body gives you signals please pay attention! It's letting you know that something is wrong. I couldn't see everything that's going on inside me.

Daughter

My princess, my daughter, the birth of her was beautiful the pain that a mother goes through baring her child is a blessing. My daughter I love her so much she is like a precious jewel you will never know how much I loved this little girl. I took her through so much where as her grandmother and my sister had to take care of her. There wasn't a book to tell you how to be a mother I love my daughter with all my heart, I made a lot of mistakes being so young it was hard but I tried. When I got to a point where I couldn't take care of my child I felt like I was having a nervous breakdown. I asked for help, thank God that I did have family to help me or else she would have went into the system. When you're using drugs it's hard to cope, people drink alcohol and drugs to suppress the pain that they are feeling, after it's all over the pain is still there and you get more depressed and you want more drugs. As years went on my daughter and I talked about my drug use how I had no respect for her how I put man before her, and a lot of women do that today even if they're not drugging because their self-esteem is shot. It took a long time-years for my child to even say I love you again. I thought after I got clean that everything will be okay, not so. She had a rough life I had a man in my life that would beat me up because I wouldn't give them my check, or I wouldn't get out in the street so that he can pimp me. If I had **to dance** in the streets it sure didn't go to a man, I used it for myself and my child. I got high in front of my daughter she used to yell at me and say, what are trying to do, kill yourself; I would just look at her and say go to your room.

I had friends we got high all the time, when the drugs was gone and the money too and you sitting there looking stupid and paralyzed, in my head wondering what the hack am I going to do. This particular day I got so sick and tired of being high I called my job, I tried to call out sick, but my boss said, gets your butt dress take a shower and get in here to work. I was so paranoid to leave the house I jumped in the shower got dressed caught the bus and went to work. When I arrived she took me in the office and asked me what my problem was. I cried out help me, she got me help, and she stated that my attitude towards the patient's coworkers was not right it was very unprofessional. **I used to sniff so much cocaine back in the day,** my coworker that I used to get a ride home with told me I was a dressed up addict. I told him to get out my face, he told me to just come with him somewhere I didn't have to say anything but listen. When I arrived at the gym where they was holding a meeting I got scared, I sat down and when they went around the room to identify their self but when it came to me I just said I am a visitor and they said sister keep coming. At that time I realized they had the same problem as I did and worse, I went into rehab for seven days and then outpatient services. I stay clean and started back again. I asked her to forgive me that time as I knew it would take time. It was a long healing process I use to drive to Brooklyn and cop some drugs. My girlfriend and I, one day we went in this building meeting with these guys they pull out a 22 and put them to our heads and told us not to turn around for 15 minutes or they would kill us. Honey we waited until 20 minutes scared as you know what! After we left shaking like a leaf, the next couple of days we went right back to NYC but a different area, that's what the drugs do to you, at one time I stayed with my mom selling drugs out of her house she couldn't believe it, even this day it's hard for her to swallow that pill about me, drugs make you do crazy things. Daughter, I ask for you to forgive me, time and time she wrote me the most beautiful poems because you are my mother and I read it over and over. My beautiful daughter I can't express enough how sorry I am for hurting you for putting you through so much pain and misery all I can ask is that you forgive me and we go on from here. Life is so short. For people who have children today is a blessing from God, for people who still have a mother cherish her, and a dad we only have one in this world each and every day because once they're gone there gone.

Can't get another No matter if you have a Godmother, favorite auntie, People who have sisters and brothers, now and then there are those who wish they had siblings, and the ones who do have siblings; don't "appreciate them." I wish today I was as close to my siblings like sisters should be, but we are not, my mother always wanted four girls in which she had three beautiful daughters and 1 son. I still pray that one day it will be possible for us to come as one; we serve an awesome God, and if it's his will before she leaves this earth it will happen. Our children today forget that we a once was their age and won't tell them anything wrong, you can raise them and let them go, they have their own minds and pray that they raise their children the right way, not by buying clothes and sneakers that is not going to work or try to be their friend instead of their parents, love your children the best you know how, hug them, try to listen to see what they have to say. It is very important today, try to help our children, it starts from home, we are there role model. At lease I own up to what I did, some people still can't accept or take on their responsibility, you have to be true to yourself so that you may move on, believe me it wasn't easy, I no longer wear the mask that I use too, this is the real me.

I feel good in my own skin knowing that I accept who I am today and don't try to be or act like someone else, I feel free and good about me being confident and strong, I know today everyone will not like me or accept me, don't' let them steal your joy, God made all of us different because we all are unique in our own way. Today parents don't do that and that's where the mistake comes in. Our children need good role models, I never had one but if I could be one to someone today I would do so. I made a lot of mistake in my life I don't regret them it was a lesson learned. The drugs had me so messed up I couldn't think right I use to walk the Streets of NYC knowing I had family across the water, but my pride and I was embarrassed. People was already talking I didn't want to hear the truth from anyone at that time I wasn't ready. I kept relapsing until I had enough, no matter who or what people say it won't work until you, and yourself is sick and tired of living that way. I learned the hard way that to be my own best friend, because there's going to be days where no one is going to be there for me. I have come through many storms, thanks to God. He has made me a strong woman but every once in a while I would like someone to take my hand and say Princess, everything is going to be alright. Just this year I started seeing a therapist for the domestic violence in my life it came a time in my life where I couldn't deal with what had happen to me so long ago, because I pushed it way back in my mind, but I was a prisoner in my own apartment, I was afraid to go out, when I did I had to pray because I didn't know if I would run into this guy. It was God's grace and mercy that brought me through

This storm, when I saw the therapist for the first time I cried through the whole session I couldn't stop, it was the first time in about 15 years that I finally dealt with it. I finally felt so good to let that pain out, I felt like my heart was lifted and the weight was gone, thank you Jesus. My boyfriend at the time I meet him in California, I was going through so much pressure I figured moving would be good for me, my older sister had temporary custardy of my child, I was still getting high at this time, it was so bad that she told the school not to let me see my child, I would come to the playground and watch her through the fence, and cry. I loved her so much but I knew I couldn't take care of her at the time. I was so unhappy and miserable down in the dumps not being with her, one day my daughter caught me crying, I tried to explain to her that I couldn't take care of her, the little voice on the other end of the phone kept saying mommy I love you, I just want to be with you, mom, I don't care what you going through. She didn't understand, so I had a plan, I told my mom and sister I wanted to move to California, they said, you can't even take care of yourself, well I wanted my little girl with me and she wanted to be with me no matter what I was going through. She couldn't understand, it broke my heart to hear her crying mommy I don't care I just want to be with you, so I made it happen so we could be together. It was her birthday coming up, at that time I was dating a detective and I asked him how would it work if I was to take my daughter from my sister, he said nothing because I was her mother. Now if it happen in this day and time they would have the AMBER Alert, but back then I didn't have to worry about that, it broke my heart looking through the playground fence at my child and couldn't talk to her and hold her. I was really mess up in the head, so I put my plan into motion. I wasn't that crazy, I prayed

Chyna Doll

to God to guide me I needed her in my life just because you are going through trails and tribulation doesn't me you are off your rocker. They call me the black sheep of the family, it hurt every time they would say oh she didn't take her medicine, but I just prayed to God because I knew in my heart I had more sense than them. But to hear them keep saying she crazy and need medicine hurts. So I said let's see how crazy they really think I was when I pull this one off, who will get the last laugh?

That weekend I called my sister and begged her to let me come and get my daughter for the birthday weekend, girl I know you are up to something. I convinced her that I wasn't up to anything so please let me have my daughter for her birthday. Finally she did said yes. I advised my baby girl she who was only four years of age, I promise her that once I get her she would never have to go there ever again. We both started crying because she would tell me how she would get spankings while she was wet. I said baby can you keep a secret; she said yes mommy I just want to be with you, my heart was hurting so bad. I said to her no matter how much they pick on you, no matter how much they make you mad you can't say anything ok. I said baby girl just pick out two of your best toys, and when we get to where we going I will buy you more. She said ok we had two more weeks before her birthday, that Friday when I pick her up I was scared, but it infuriated me because of what I had to go through to get my little girl. We had made it safely to California. I did contact her and my mother after we arrived in California several months later. I didn't say where we was but I did let my daughter speak to them and she let them know she was happy to be with me. After 2 months I finally said do you guys want to have lunch? They said yes, I laughed and said it will be an expensive lunch, my mom said are you in NYC, I said no we are in California, she said Leslie called the police on you, I told her there was nothing they could do to me I checked it out before I made my move, and I am her mother, therefore nothing they could do.

Now if it was today and I tried something like that the Amber Alert would have been a problem for me. I thank God I had my daughter and we were safe together. The first night was very hard for the both of us; we both cried happy tears and sad ones because of how I had to go about getting my child back with me. Then I got out there and had two jobs to put her in school she was so more advanced than the children in her class, but we made it work. At the time it got a little rough because Silky was doing his thing and it wasn't a good one and I didn't want to fall by the way side with him. I tried to help him pull out but you can't help someone if they are not ready. So I kept doing me and taking care of business so that I can get an apartment. It took 6 months to 1 year finally I got an apartment, moved out and Silky and I stay in touch. I met this crazy guy name Dale, like a lot of women we see the signs but I ignore them. Well he was an artist and I met him in a club, he was very over protective, controlling and unpredictable, as time went on he got bossy and tried to keep me away from my friends. Dale was very jealous, if I was dancing or sitting at a table I couldn't look at no one but him…For a minute I'm saying to myself, I said nah this isn't happening to me, but yes it was. He use to bring home women and draw there portrait and wouldn't let me in. I would be fuming and when he got finished we would argue and fight. It went on for a couple of years, and then I started drugging again. It got so bad my daughter wasn't happy and she would run away. He wanted me to be a lady of the night, I said are you freaking crazy that was another fight because I wouldn't do it. I didn't care what he wanted that was out of my character. What I did do was caught the bus to this club, I knew the owner and had a drink and ask him to get me a ticket to go back home, he said yes. So, I sent my daughter back first with her father who was supposed to pick her up from the airport but never

A Girl with Nine Lives

did, so my mom and sister did. I was on the wrath path because he never showed and his mother wouldn't take her, my Jess said she would keep her, but the oldest wouldn't let her stay. I never mentioned to my mom, well you know she wouldn't have believed her or me if I told her why I didn't want her to go back to Leslie's house. Well she wind up going back with Leslie, and crying out for me and I wasn't there for her. A couple of weeks later I caught a bus back to Maryland I couldn't take the abuse any more. One day I waited for him to leave and when he left, I went back to my girlfriend's house but he would stalk me outside her house I was scare to death. I would go back home with him and he would make me have sex with him, I was so afraid of him I did it. I believe it was emotional and physical abuse, unfortunately I overlooked it in the beginning but it started getting worst. He would sabotage my jobs showing up unannounced, calling all the time. Humiliated, I felt powerless. Finally my friend got me a ticket to travel back home, I was so grateful I waited until he left the house and went to catch the Greyhound bus back home, I was mortified and ashamed but I got on that bus. I left everything behind just took a few clothes. So that it would look like I was coming back to the apartment. Ladies we have to put a plan in motion and act on it, because that is not love, its abuse. While

Chyna Doll

we were together we took a trip to Maryland, and went to see my sister Jess, she was in the hospital at the time. I came home to visit her, he remembered where she lived he knew she was my favorite sister. So a couple of years went by and I haven't heard from him for a minute. But he didn't forget me leaving him the way I did.

So couple of years pass and I heard a knock at my sisters door, I happen to be there at the time, I open the door up it was Dale, I was surprise to see him he had a plan for me that I didn't even know, he set me up real good he was very nice too and said let me take you to dinner? So I mention it to my sister she said don't go, I said girl he can't do anything to me knowing that I haven't seen this man in a couple of years; since I left him was planning to get back at me but I didn't think so, his behavior was very normal at first then he change like Dr, Jekyll and Mr. Hide, this is the circle of domestic violence, but I didn't know that at the time, so I went with him any way ignoring the little voice inside me, honey, Ladies when that voice inside you, tell you or warn you; we need to listen, but we don't, well we went to New York City had a beautiful dinner, then we went back to his hotel room and made passionate love, next thing I knew I was sitting on the edge of the bed he snap, he said to me woman. I am going to kill you, my eyes got so big, I said my sister know that I am with

A Girl with Nine Lives

you, he said she will never fine you, my heart stating beating really fast, he took my clothes and pocket book and through them out the window, then he punch me in the face blacken my eye bust my lips, I was crying saying why, why, he said woman you left me and think you so fine, I cry harder, he said it's too late I am going to kill you, I ask to go to the bathroom he said go ahead he stood in the door way, he said hurry up, now I am looking around to see how I can get out of there, we were on the 11th floor, no way out of the window, so he watch me while I walk back in the room sat on the bed got punch again in the face after a while I couldn't even see, he made me have sex with him for hours after while my body was numb, while we were having sex he kept hitting me in my face. I beg and pleaded with him how sorry I was for leaving him, he call me all kind of names the guy in the room next, nock on our door, and said is everything ok over her, Dale, said yes that's just my wife she's crazy, the guy said ok, then dale shut the door, that made him beat me some more, when they say your life flash before your eyes, it does, he had me on my back and was on top of me, all I could do is think about my daughter I will never see her again, he had some of his artist material on the bed I could barely see out of one eye, I thought that this only happens in the movies, but it was real; and it was happing to me right then, I pray to

God so hard that this man was really trying to kill me and I didn't want to die, so I reach over my right arm while he was on top of me, grab the scissors in my hand held them real tight grip; and stab him in the back that he had to get off of me. I hurry unchain the door and ran and jump down 2-3 stairs at a time to the lobby for help, when I finally got there, people was surprise to see me and the manager took me to the back I ask the guy when he comes down asking for me to say I ran out the door, no sooner than I said that he came down asking did they see me, they said she ran out the door, he said how she couldn't when she wasn't wearing anything. The desk clerk convenience him I had left and ran out the door, my ankles was so swallow I couldn't walk, the guy next door came running downstairs and said where she is I heard her screaming, I felt like I was in a twilight zone, I couldn't stop crying the guys said why, why you didn't say anything I would have help you, I said he threaten my child, I was petrified, hysterical and horrified, he look at me and said he needs someone to beat him up, I was in bad shape He pick me up carry me up stairs to his room wash me up and then sat me on the bed, and said you are so fine that I just have to do you, I look at him in a outrage and offended, I had already been tortured enough, and now this man wants to rape me, I look at him with my eyes half open and said you know; my body is numb I can't feel anything so if that's what you want to do to me then go ahead. I was powerless wasn't anything I could do. I asked him to get me some clothes and shoes to wear and a hat? After he finishes with me I fell to sleep and woke up very early, He brought me a pair of 9 sneaker, I wear a 6 ½, and these big jeans and a big man's sweater,

And a wool cap. Oh my; I cry some more then he try to comfort me, gave me money to catch the train from NYC. well I differently look like a New Yorker, like I live on the streets of NY, well I was walking like a clown because the sneakers was so big on my feet I couldn't help it, I pull the wool cap all the way down over my face, so that you couldn't see it, I walk from time square to 33rd street path train, got on the train got to Penn Station Newark, I call a girlfriend that worked night so she had just got home from the night shift, I call her and said, Ann can you please come and pick me up from Penn Station, I never told her what happen to me, she said girl I am tired I can't I just got in from work; and I hung up the phone. Then, started crying again, I look around to make sure I didn't see any one I knew, my ankles was hurting so bad when I walked because they was so swallow, I pray to God to help me make to my sister's house, I said Lord I don't have any money I can't barely walk please help me to get to my sister's. I started walking the back streets to the project praying that I don't ran into anyone because people was going to work that early, as I arrive at the project's, I ran into a guy name Mac, he knew, I try to ignore him, but he kept looking like he knew me, I was walking with my head down but he knew it was me. He stops and said? What happen to you? I answer please take me to my sister's house.

Please don't ask me a question right now; he then proceeded to take me by the hand and escorted me to my sisters, I said to him when he knock on her door to tell her don't get upset when she see me, he knock she answer, he said I have your sister Princess, here on the side but please don't get upset, she said where is she, I came up the stairs and she stared cursing when she saw me; and said I ask you not to go with him, I said please just let me take a bath and lie down and she did, when I got up I told her he through all my clothes and pocket book out the hotel window. I had no money and clothes to wear; he was really trying to kill me. It was God Grace and Mercy that I came through this horrible experience. Today I don't know where he is, and I pray to God that I don't have to live in fear today. I just dealt with this situation with a therapist this year; it has helped a lot I cried the hold session, because I never really spoke about it. And didn't think I was going to make it, you see things like that on TV but never in my wildest dream though that it would happen to me, you just never know, people there are so many different signs of abuse, my x-husband never knew about this incident I was too embarrassed to tell him and didn't want to live it all over again there is emotional abuse, Physical abuse, Economic or Financial Abuse. The abuser uses a variety of tactics, for instinct, they will dominance, Humiliate you in public, threat you, try to Isolation you. The abuser is very dangerous please women and men look out for the signs, there is help out there today you don't have to live in silence and suffer, don't let the abuser make you feel unwanted, or your self esteem is low or you can't make it without them, because you can. I just want to give you a couple of signs, one humiliate, two criticize you all the time, three belittling you even in public, Control and excessively jealous, can go on and on, people we know, don't act like you don't know; they will trap you, pray and get the courage to reach out because people whose partner abuse them physically and emotional wine up killing you. Ladies even if your spouse forces you to have sex and you say no that is abuse as well, sexually are at a high risk of being seriously injured or killed. A couple years I was in NYC having dinner I saw the guy that help me that night but I didn't say anything and he didn't remember me, I didn't want to explain to my x-husband, at the time what happen to me. He never knew about this incident and I never told him it happen before his time. Let go, is a process for me how to let go means removing all my attention from a particular experience or a person. My pass is my pass but also joy, the struggles; I can see the possibilities my future is offering Me., in my head is still thinking about what was, I have to let it go; in order to do so, I must trust in God and have faith that the good will prevail, in spite of appearances ease the process.

I must let each experience end, whether it is good or bad, I know that all my experiences contributes to my growth, you only have one life to live and each day is a blessing, I can see how and understand as the months and the years pass how painful it was; but play a big part in my life. Attitude toward the lesson I learn life has offered me all the different in the world. Life is a challenge; life is what you make it. I understand today my ideas I couldn't gasps, but my pass may had come to terns over the years, slowly giving ways getting ready for the truth. I couldn't' absorb yesterday, the truth, it comes to me today is not always going to make me a happy person I am traveling a road that is very rocky, but I give the direction I need to go on. I learn that growing up you put people first, I've choose

A Girl with Nine Lives

to do something about the situation I'm in, I stop for a moment and I reflect on many changes in my life it's so exciting along the way because I am trusting my inner feeling and helping people along my journey I realize my heart is pure if I can seek guidance.

42nd Street New York City, I use to work over there on 42nd street just to make Extra money, my sister use to say girl where you going? I would say just out for a while; I was a little hustler; you don't always have go to bed with someone it always other ways to make money. to use your body, some time words is more powerful, most of the time I use to talk the slick talk my way out of things, over there you can work in the booths and the customers can't touch you, I love that made out good too, it only lasted for a while but I enjoyed the money until I had a stalker. Now every time I had martial affairs that didn't work out, I know it was wrong being the other women, but sometimes you need help and sometimes it not worth it, married men are like sugar daddy's they will give money buy you things, but when it comes to holidays you are on your own, because they are with their families, and they are not leaving there wives. They feel if you are a needed person they will really take advance age it is not worth it, Ladies these married men only want sex maybe a conversation, tell you they don't sleep in the same bed with her, or were not speaking she doesn't love him anymore, anything to get in your pants, don't fall for it, they know all the right word to say or do, I really felt bad but guess what it happen to me after I got married, my husband cheat on me. The 80/ 20 rule the wife still gets the 80 the mistress gets, 20. Why play yourself cheap when everything they promise you once you get a job you can buy it yourself. Whatever you want and don't have to do any favors. Everyone wants to be love but is not the way to go, remember you can do whatever you put your mind to. Don't look for love in the wrong place, pray is the best Armor!!! We women today deserve better don't play yourself short, it's not worth it the game is the same it's the players that change; they are in jail or dead, but the answer is to just wait on the Lord he will supply all of our need, that is what I had to learn. Wait on him in his time he will put someone in your life not when you want it, when he is ready. You know the pass is a lesson the present is a gift and the future is motivation and no relationship is sunshine but 2 people can share on umbrella weather the storm if they want. It was hard for me to trust again, but I am learning to love again and learning to open the door and let down my guard again, I do ask for help when need it, I am not ashamed that doesn't mean you are stupid, everyone need help one time or another. I also learned what God has bless

A Girl with Nine Lives

me with, sometimes I feel like I am not where I should be, but God said this is where I should be right now. I accept what God has done for me in my life, because without him I wouldn't be here to write my story, I am so grateful and bless. I also learning to listen more now than I did before, God, has brought me a mighty long way, when I wake up in the mornings and my eyes are open, my heart is beating God's warm blood running through my veins, it is a gift, there is power in his blood of Jesus, and honey I am a testimony....... Friends I am a survivor.

This particular morning I woke up getting ready for work, I walk in the bathroom to brush my teeth, my stomach blew up and went back down and I grab on to the sink, it was like something in the movies, I stood there for a moment then continue getting ready For work, well I got to work for about an hour I started feeling weak told my boss what had happen and they call 911, well got to the hospital my gallbladder had rupture, oh my, the reason why it didn't kill me, it was only God, again he kept me the doctor said Ms. you are lucky the poison didn't leak in my system he couldn't explain. I know it was the work of God, even though I wasn't doing the right things he still kept me again. I have two friend name Danger and Silky Smooth they have been my friend for over 20 some years, they are like the movie Chucky never go away, they been there for me through thick and thin and I thank both for their friendship, I met Danger back when I was selling Mary Kay products and coordinating weddings he works for a famous designer so whenever my brides or bridesmaids needs or someone Needed a cocktail dress or grown. We all want someone in our life to share there is a shortest of men, Silky we go way back we are family, I rather deal with men any day then women, they are so petit. A friend; a real friend is someone you love trusts and going to tell you all the things you don't want to hear about yourself, they will tell you when you're right when you're wrong, and help you understand, they will not lie to you they know your secrets and hold them in confidence never judge me yet let me know my mistakes without covering them up, steer me in the right direction they will push me, shout me, and drive me real hard just when you think you're about to break. They will wipe you off get out of the band-aid and patch you up and start pushing again. I love Danger and Silky they see right through my crap, they are someone I can look at and know that I am really going to be all right. I love these guys dearly, there comes a time in my life when I realize who matters or who don't or who never Did, and who always will be there; and I don't feel sorry about the people from my past there is a reason why they didn't make it to my future. I don't waste my precious energy on gossip or issues in the past, negative thoughts I can't control instead invest in positive present moments. Life isn't fair but still good I don't compare my life with others they have no idea of what my journey was all about. Life is too short wasted time hating people, I don't have time to win every argument, Agree to or disagree I don't worry about what other people think of me. However, a bad situation it will change the feeling in being envy, is waste of time, I asked God to make sure before I do what clutters out my mine to bed each night for my blessing, my health trends and guidance, I tried to say I will accomplish the next day. Sometimes we can complicate our life by taking on today, I don't need anyone approval of my efforts, my appearance, my aspiration and behavior. it is not normal all the time it's certainly not healthy, In my early childhood I was taught to obey and respect others, I feel we confuse love with approval and march to someone else song, Personal freedom means choosing your behavior and acting, rather the reacting. Allowing myself to for full adventure of living each moment, we all have a unique part to play we all need the almighty God in our life each and every day, I won't let no one control my action today, God will have the approval. You know what brother me most of the time as months and years go by, the problem is that whenever I think about the abuse within, there is a reasonable solution, it's also probable feared that I couldn't simply survive the complexity of any situation, but I did, Glory to God… not saying that I deserve what happen to me because no one deserve any kind of abuse, God don't give you more then you can handle, In fact I am given what I need at this time to heal, I still have many lesson to learn, that situation seem like it was something in a movie, in which you never would think that it would happen to you. I thank God for the 12 steps programs to bring me through my storm, to guide me it's still hard sometime but I keep praying, I mainly remember what I am powerless over that there is a Higher Power then myself, that life will become simply when I can accept the things I can't change.

But then today, I believe there are eight qualities of a women, this is my prospected – *Beauty, to be yourself, wisdom, making right choices, Happiness, Harmony, Balance your life, Courage, mean what you say and stick to it, be strong, Generosity, don't let people take advantage, know yourself.*

You know sometimes I thought I would lose mine, but God kept me. There was times when I thought I couldn't go on or live without someone in my life, then there was a time when I wanted to just lash out at those who hurt me but God kept me, God kept my mouth shut.

In my recovery, I had to apologize to the many people I hurt. It was very hard but in order to heal, I had to do it. My mom, until today, can't believe the things that I did, but mom knows I wasn't an angle.

For my daughter, again, I don't know how many times I can apologize to you. I am thankful for your grandmother and my sister for taking care of you because I wasn't well.

A lot of people misjudge me and misunderstood me, but under all my pain and suffering, I always believe we all make wrong choices in our lives. I know God changes people because he changed me. I pray that these words will be recorded in every heart and every eye that see me and every mouth that can confess willingly. I am kept afloat by my past, but that is just a preview. That is just an introduction. I am safe on my raft, but I can't help the feeling of wanting to get off. I can swim but I should attempt to walk in the current that is my life. The raft is breaking from under me and the water in coming in. There is a rock in my thought that has smashed my raft. Now, I am floating on my back, drifting in to my emotion, awakened on a safe land, surrounded in tranquility. I am in a quit, calm river kept by the clean air of my future, relaxing on the raft of my present.

I just want to say it was a long and hard journey. It was a light at the end of the tunnel. A couple of years ago, I had a mild stroke. I didn't even know that was happening to me but again, God kept me. I felt good that morning, took a shower but before that I had a headache for a couple of days, I slip on some sweats and started crying, walked across the hall and told my neighbor I was having a heart attack. She medially called 911. She and the boyfriend stayed with me until the EMS arrived. Hallelujah!!! Glory to God! Again, he kept me. God is still using me. I can't question it. I don't understand it but I am grateful for his grace and mercy and to say that we serve an awesome God. I thank him each and every day of my life, whatever his purpose is for me. I will serve him the best that I can.

Even when I was in the streets, people thought they could take advantage of me. It had a lot to do with my past - the drugs but I wasn't out of it that I didn't know what someone was saying to me or asking me. I will never forget when I was standing outside at James's, talking to some friends selling drugs, my uncle came up to me and said, *"Let's trade."* I said, *"Trade what?"* He walked with a limp. I curse him out and said don't get it twisted; don't let this petty face fool you. I immediately went up stairs and told my mom what he had said to me, she just look at me, like I was crazy, and I walked away.

People that is what's wrong with our parents today. Please listen to your children. They will not lie to you about someone touching them, or try to do something to them, because it is always a friend and family member. I never spoke to that man again. When I was in the streets, I knew who to talk and who to mess with. I didn't have to do favors if I didn't want to, and some people wanted me too. I was in control of me beside the devil inside of me. Today, I am in a good place. I moved to another State with my niece. I love her so much; she has supported me through everything. Ms. P, I love you to pieces. I finally got my life together. I found a new church home and I am back on the right path. I asked God to forgive me for my sins, and I pray if my story could help one person.

I am grateful. It wasn't easy writing about me. It became a healing process for me, because I had to relive my life all over again, it was very painful. I am retired now, but still a volunteer at Women for Domestic Violence in NYC with my friend. I love you, man. Thank for your love and support. Also to Ms. P, thank you, for being patient with me. I want to give honor to God who's the head of my life for allowing me to write my story and tell the truth about what happened to me.

I am not ashamed of what I went through. It was a learning experience but I don't wish it to happen to anyone else. Living in silent will drive you nuts, but I had God in my life that kept me sane. If you were to meet me for the first time, you wouldn't be able to see the scars, but I had them and live with them for 60 years. I never wanted to go back to that lifestyle ever, God willing.

I remember when my daughter used to ask me when I got depress or feeling down, did I feel like getting high? I look at her and said, *"Baby, I know what it did to you and me, with the grace of God I never want to relive that life, I've came a long way and still have a long way to go."*

I pray to God that he will keep me on the right path. Every day, when I wake up, before my feet hit the floor, I sit up and say, *thank you Lord for another day.*

There is no special way to pray. You just talk to God like you are talking to a friend and he will hear your pray. It doesn't have to be anything fancy, just tell him want you are thinking and feeling. I thank him for my eyes opening up.

I just want to say if you can trust someone and you're in trouble, please reach out. no one deserve to be abused. If you can't talk to anyone or trust them or not, writing how you feel will give you so much relief until you get the courage to reach out, and differently pray.

God will hear your cry for help. I know he heard mine. God Bless. When we don't know who we are, it is easy to compromise ourselves and when we don't know where we stand on an issue, values may be cloudy in our minds. We may not be aware of them at all. It's then that we are vulnerable to be persuasion to someone. We will find happiness when we learn to get quiet and listen to our inner self. We will find it when we learn to focus our personal problem and more on other people needs. I can expect to feel fear at times, even dread it, some situation at times seem more than I can handle. But it is said we could only bear what is given to us. I've learn that it shall pass also, my confident Grew spiritual, and gain strength. I am truly grateful for my growth in the Lord today; still have a long way to go, and the opportunities that lie ahead. My strength carries me through trouble times, if it wasn't for God, but my memory fails me. I try to solve the problem then stumble to determine the proper course. Relying on God with my life encourages me. I understand God presence is foreign to my life, for a early childhood when my courage fail as sometimes it did, I hid in fear, I get down on my knees and pray, I can't let go, I can't let the devil destroy me, I Need to be still and listen for that conversation from God.

*G*iving honor to God who is the head of my life thank you allowing me to write my story, I pray that it may reach someone out there, It is help today, I give God all the Glory and Honor because I couldn't have got through this storm by myself, I knew this guy and he use to say it was him that made him the way he was, he didn't understand that there is a Amazing God that helps him until he got sick, I say that, You can't make on your own today, we need God everyday in our life. And guest who he call out too, God. I am saying that if you don't know God, please get to know him because he Love you and will get you through whatever your situation is.

We Sever Awesome God!!!!!!! As it is said in Philippians 4:13 I can do all things through Christ who strengthens me. Hallelujah!!! Glory to God…..

Printed in the United States
By Bookmasters